Still Tilting at Windmills

Peter Lay

Black Eyes Publishing UK

Still Tilting at Windmills
By Peter Lay
© Peter Lay, 2019

Published by Black Eyes Publishing UK, 2019
Brockworth, Gloucestershire, England
www.blackeyespublishinguk.co.uk

ISBN: 978-1-9999583-5-0

Peter Lay has asserted his moral right under the Copyright, Designs and Patents Act, 1988, to be identified as the author of this work.

All Rights reserved. No part of this publication may be reproduced, copied, stored in a retrieval system, or transmitted, in any form or by any means, without the prior written consent of the copyright holder, nor be otherwise circulated in any form of binding or cover other than that in which it is published and without a similar condition being imposed on the subsequent purchaser.

A CIP catalogue record for this title is available from the British Library.

Edited by: Josephine Lay

Cover design: Jason Conway, cre8urbrand.
www.cre8urbrand.co.uk

Also, by Peter Lay & Zaiming Wang

Yellow Over The Mountain
岭上黄

Another Friday

~

Also, By Peter Lay

redbootsman 'Such Strange Philosophies'

In a quiet room
I sat eating my breakfast
And listening to the sound
Of my inner thoughts

The process was like
Sitting before still water
And watching the ripples spread
From a dropped pebble

I chose a smooth stone
Unblemished and spherical
It felt perfect in my hand
A truth worth keeping

And yet I slipped it
Into the depths of my mind
And felt the ripples wash through
My preconceptions

Josephine Lay, April 2018

Index

Don Quixote	11
Words	12
First Draft	13
One becomes Two	14
Friday Morning	15
Peace	16
Stuff	17
Wriggle	18
Fallen Angels	19
Last Post	20
Hand	22
Quito Climate	23
Tongues	24
Kama Sutra	25
Close to Me	26
Gusting	27
Warmer	28
Wind	29
Where did the Heat Go	30
Love	31
Sometimes	32
Ode to my Younger Self	34
I hope you are continuing to mend…	35
Expectation	36
As shadows block your way	37
Maria	38
Mist of Time	40
Japan (November 2018)	41
~ Nagasaki	43
~ Nerium Oleander	46
~ Naoshima	50
~ Miyajima	53
~ A Japanese Garden	54

Everything	57
The Bear	58
As	59
Know	60
Daydreaming	61
Turquoise	62
Hug	63
Beauty	64
Smile	65
Blue Skies	66
In my hotel	67
Avebury	68
Revolution	69
Shit	70
Brick	71
Here	72
Death	73

Still Tilting at Windmills

Don Quixote

Where is my horse?

I am a knight
But my armour is rusty
And my trusty steed
And my knight's shoes, I need...
Are missing

So, as I begin my quest
To rescue a princess
I'm sat on a rock
Where I'm taking stock

I am in a line
From Don Quixote
Still tilting at windmills
In dreams...

Words

Words are spinning through my mind
Backwards and forwards, and some in rhyme
Me they say, whilst jockeying for position
We can deliver, your feelings, this time

We can play it, centre stage
Strap on a guitar and begin to strum it
We feel the rhythm and begin to play it
We find the tune and begin to hum it

The words are dancing into vision
The opening line, is their mission
The smoke rises; it becomes clear
I'm actually singing in my lover's ear

First Draft

Steps end in the water
Sounds of lapping
I reach for the handrail
As the odour of summer
Makes me drink
From the cool bottle

I make red slashes on squares
Looking for structure

Tables for standing
Intense conversation
I lift the cup
Smell the flavour
Before the taste

Disjointed words
Take me back
Every face behind the mask
Echoes of ghosts
From the past

I see you
I hear you
I reach for you
I sense your perfume
Before I inhale it

I want to read it… Venice

One becomes Two

It is likely to be a cold wet day
Today, this Saturday
And overnight
Tonight
We lose an hour
As one becomes two
In the cold...

Friday Morning

I am a little concerned
With talk of death
And I know what you say
Is just logic in a way

But me, I am immortal
So I've always thought
I cannot imagine
Giving up my mortal coil

So, I am a little concerned
With this talk of death
Is there more for me to know
About your lasting health

Peace

Find peace in sleep,
free from anxiety
and fear

Tomorrow is another day
Another day for people
to find a way
to live in peace
and harmony

Stuff

Always stuff to deal with
Sisters digging in heels
Wives falling off theirs
Water coming through ceilings
Ice packs wrapped around legs
And the heat
slows us little by little
as we shuffle from place to place
Obligations
Responsibilities
We want to scream
and shout
instead of laughing
Dancing
Kissing
Loving
Our lives are filled
Dealing with stuff...

Wiggle

Come to me my love
Fill my life with passion
Entice me with your lips
And a wiggle of your hips

The whisper on your thighs
of the swish of your skirt
Something to savour
As my senses alert

Nothing compares to you
As in our arms we press
Hearts beating in unison
Your breasts against my chest

Fallen Angels
Peter Lay & Josephine Lay

Fallen angels tear at my flesh
Tormenting me to lust…
Talons scratch across my chest
Burning my soul in devilish fire
And cremating my flesh to dust…
Although I'll perish, I would not stop
This exquisite agony…
They have me body, mind and soul
And I can never be free

Fallen angels with hair of jet
And skin of alabaster
Blood red lips and teeth so sharp,
Eyes that glint with fire…
I will succumb to your deadly kiss
That draws my entirety…
Drowning in waves of bliss
Until my life grows old
I have no wish to be free

Cover me, smother me
In caresses sweet and sharp
Oh, fallen angels with icy hearts
Piercing my mouth with tongues of fire
Leave me no hope of life to come
I'll perish happily in this desire…
Tread on my dreams
Till reality ceases to be
Only then, will I be free of thee

Last Post

There we were laying in bed
Discussing the things
That come in our heads

Josephine, I said
'The man'
Clive Oseman, 'the man'
Is going to Covent Garden
To Sylvia Plath poetry
What is that?

You may not know
But she and I
Are fans of long dead youthful poets?
Many of whom
Went too soon…
Sylvia, 30, suicide
Anne Sexton, 46, suicide
And Woodpecker
That's Takuboku Ishigawa, 26, TB
To name but three…

Misuzu Kaneko, 27, suicide
That makes four…

Dylan Thomas, 39, pneumonia
And the famous trio of English romantics
Keats, 26, TB
Byron, 36, bled to death by himself and doctors
Shelley, 30, drowned or murdered?
Adds some more…

I saw a post, I spout
On Facebook
By the man, I recount

She's excited
By this post recounted
Puts down Sylvia
Really?
What is that?
Phone in hand I begin to scroll
But all I find is lots of droll
Hang on, 'the man' is a friend
So, a few clicks later
I'm on his page

Here I say, here it is
Pointing to that certain post
But as I read, the certainty drifts
My brain does a jump
The words un-jumble
And there for all to see
Is Silver Path poetry

What is that?

Senility?

Hand

Sleep on my love
Until I can
Come to your bed
And hold your hand

Kiss your lips
And make you smile
Entwine with you
For a while

Quito Climate

Sunny in the morning
Cloudy for lunch
Rain in the afternoon
Cold at night

Tongues

My tongue
Your tongue
Loving
Inside a kiss

Kama Sutra

This way and that
Put your leg here
and your hand there
I'll lift my shoulders
as you bend one leg
that's it....
Is it good for you?

We appear to be stuck....

HELP...

Close to me

You are sleeping
So deeply
I hold you
Close to me
Feeling your heart beating
Next to mine

You are breathing
So gently
Your lips
Slightly parted
Just centimetres
From mine

Gusting

Its light here now
the rain is coming down
The wind is howling
gusting all around

Women run with billowing skirts
Failing to keep them down
Seeking shelter from the storm
Relentlessly lashing down

Warmer

Seems it's getting warmer,
And the snow is melting...
A few days and it will be gone...
Women will undo their coats,
To reveal their tight dresses,
And short skirts...
In the hope of being noticed...

Wind

As the snow recedes
The sting in its tail
Seeps into you
Freezing taut nipples

This northern invader,
Blinds our eyes
The sting in its tail,
Beware its bite

Where did the heat go?

Where did the heat go?
Once more the world
Has become cold and damp…

Where did the sun go?
Little summer dresses
Hidden under wet
Raincoats…

Love

My body naked
Cold and shivering
Pressed against the window pane
Where rivers run down the glass
Driven by rain

Sometimes

As I write upon the page
The words
They splutter from my brain
Sometimes they make sense
At others not at all
But here I am
Pen in hand all the same

Sometimes I get a line
Sometimes two or three
'Genius' I think
But there it stops
My hand flops
The pen I drop
No more words will come to me
At this moment I cannot see
Inseminated
The wood for the many trees

What shall I say?
What words should I write?
At times like these
Nothing
Zilch
Nani mo
Méiyǒu
Nada
Rien
The connections in my brain
Splutter
Falter
Disconnect
Frustrated I turn away

Looking out the window
Through the drops of rain
Careering across the pane of glass
At the sodden garden
Did I say it is raining?
Cos it is… Non-stop...
'I don't have WhatsApp', I hear her say
Through the pitter patter
'What's that?'

I'm thinking
That's enough of this drivel
As I gaze through the rivel-
let's of rain on the window
From the sun there is no glow
So, it's time to go
Stop looking out the window
Let's watch Qi and go to bed…

Goodbye

Ode to my Younger Self

Live
Don't Wait
Time is ticking
Till when
No one knows

Do it now
Find a way
Go with the wind
Wherever it takes you
Existence is all

Open your eyes and see
Understand your vision
Feel the presence
Of those you meet
Along the way

Seek those curves
In the linear landscape
Thrill at the touch
The exploration
Of sensuality

Be able to look back
And smile
No regrets
Your life is yours
Live it…

I hope you are continuing to mend...

Life,
Sometimes it is like
A weary trudge,
In a thick heavy overcoat,
Through a dank dark mire,
At others like,
Skipping carefree,
In a light summer dress,
Through a field of daisies...

I hope the sun is good for you...

Expectation

I awake
Not to the sun
But to clouds
And the expectation
Of rain

So, I look
For a smile to
Light the sky
In beautiful eyes
Reflected

As shadows block your way

As shadows block your way
your guards deserting
leave you vulnerable
to sudden attack

It is time to regroup
to find another route
No less easy
and you will have to pay

Maria
(Remembering September 1990)

The telephone ringing
Pulls me awake
I answer it blearily
Shaking sleep from my head
There's a faint static on the line
As a nurse says softly 'It may be time'

I sit shaken then pick up the phone
Make frantic calls to Mother, Father, brothers and friends
Then gently waking the children
I tell them to dress
'We have to go'

She looks so peaceful
There in her bed
While patients on intravenous medication
Connected by tubes
On poles
On wheels
Are wandering around

It's not looking good
She is not able to wake
So, there we wait, by the bed
As people come and go
To say 'Hello'
And whisper 'Goodbye'

We are sitting
When afternoon comes
We leave to smoke
Or stretch our legs

We are changing shifts
Taking our turn
When a voice from the bed
Says 'What's going on?'

A reprieve to breathe
But not forever
An extra six weeks
To be together

Mist of Time

When they mess with time
They mess with my head
Confusion reigns inside my brain
But I am talking just the same

We must make a new regime
For once what was eight
Is becoming nine

So now we settle into this
Finding the way to keep our tryst
In six months' time it's back again
The hour we gained, lost in mist

Japan

Nagasaki *(Friday 9th November 2018)*

Nagasaki
I chose you first
to record my sentiments
in this verse
You who were second
Here will be first...

On the day
The crab crossed the baked sand
In front of a deep blue sea
The 'Fat Man' fell

The Fat Man
just over three metres
by one and a half metres
Weighed 4.5 tons
and was painted
bright yellow

On the ninth of August 1945
at 11:02
within one second
40,000 people die
40% of the buildings vaporise

The number of dead doubles
as the lucky survivors
begin to fall...

Nagasaki shaped like
an amphitheatre
With crooked streets
and tiered houses

clinging to the hillsides
at the mouth
of the Urakami River
For so long
the only accessible port
to the west
Utterly devastated

The Sanno Shrine
About 800 metres
from the epi-centre
was obliterated
and nearby trees disappeared…
A blackened torii gate stands
one of its columns destroyed
the remaining column
supporting the weight
of half the crosspiece
Now an icon to tourists

On that day
due to the weather
the B-29 Superfortress
'Bockscar'
was diverted from its primary target
to release its plutonium payload
to detonate at 500 metres
above Nagasaki

I stand, numbed, at the epi-centre
It is hard to imagine
that everything I can see
Me and the people I can see
And those that I can't see
In one second
would just cease to be…

My knees buckle
and I sit
Shaken by the emotion of it

What is it like to come second
in the race to destruction?
Only two cities in the world
have been devastated by nuclear attack
Nagasaki and Hiroshima
Only one country has ever
carried out a nuclear attack,
the United States of America
supported by Great Britain
to test their theories
and apparently justified by Japanese atrocities
in South East Asia
BUT
An atrocity is an atrocity
One does not justify the other

Nerium Oleander is the official flower of the city of Hiroshima. This is because it was the first flower to bloom again following the atomic bomb destruction.
Nin is Japanese for person/people.

Nerium Oleander *(Monday 12th November 2018)*

A small girl on her knees
Crying in the rain
Her memories carried in a purse

When the B-29 'Enola Gay'
Drops her 'Little Boy'
Over Hiroshima
At 8:15 on the sixth of August 1945
In the blink of an eye
70,000 nin die
And only 30% of buildings survive

A giant mushroom cloud
Billows
Carrying radioactive soot,
Dust, debris and dirt
High into the sky
Where it mixes with water vapour
And falls back to earth
As 'Black Rain'...

Many victims jump into the river
Shouting
Mizu mizu mizu
Water water water
And drown

Little Boy
Had instantaneously decimated
The entire city
Government agencies were obliterated
Transport paralysed
Yet somehow…
Support systems
Became immediately re-instated…

By the very next day
the army, Government
and citizens had set up…
First aid posts
Transport to relief stations
Cremations of the dead
and food distribution

During the subsequent
Allied occupation
US military censors
withheld news of the
dire devastation
of the atomic attacks
from the Japanese population
All the while extolling
The virtues of a free press

They supressed statistics;
A further 70,000 nin deceased
by the end of the year
They confiscated
film shot after the attacks
in Hiroshima and Nagasaki
by Japanese cameramen…
The US occupation force
through the Atomic Bomb

Casualty Commission
maintained a monopoly
on both scientific
and medical statistics...
No results were offered for relief
or treatment of the victims

2-year-old
Sadako Sasaki survived
But 9 years later
like others
she contracted leukaemia...
She folded paper cranes
Continuously
hoping
they would help her recovery
But 8 months later
she was just a memory...

There followed a movement
to build a memorial
The Children's Peace Monument
for the thousands of children
dead before their time...
Now used as a meeting point
for so many young people
in the Peace Park today

Offerings of water
in cups and bottles
are left at memorial stones
These are removed by photographers
Totally missing the point...
And yesterday
graffiti appeared...

The stone doves
in the student tower
cry for the loss of learning

I look at you and see
tears in your eyes
You break down and cry
like the small girl on her knees
crying in the rain
Her memories carried in a purse

Domo arigato gozaimasu

- *'Little Boy' - Uranium atomic bomb*

- *'A small girl on her knees
   Crying in the rain
   Her memories carried in a purse'*

   (Inspired by a scene in the Studio Ghibli anime film, 'Grave of the Fireflies', directed by Isao Takahata)

- *Peace,
   Where Japan leads
   The world might follow...*

Naoshima

From Hiroshima
take the shinkansen
to Okayama
Then the local train
to Uno Port
Lastly the ferry
to Naoshima
The island of Art

Significant spaces created
by contemporary
Art and Architecture
to resonate
with the pristine nature
of the Seto inland sea
A landscape
rich in culture and history

First take
the cramped and full
local bus
Making spaces
for large and heavy cases
on the short trip
across to Nokyo-mae
and guest house Oomiyake…

On the next day
take a hilly walk
across the island
as the sun warms the sky
amid a landscape of surprises
to the Chichu Art Museum…

Between the ticket centre
and the entrance
is the Chichu garden
designed with the images
of the scenery
that inspired Monet
His beloved flowers
trees
and the pond with water lilies
where the light changes
over the course of the day

No photography
inside the museum
But a picture
could do no justice
where the entire museum
becomes an Art space

Five paintings by Monet
In a space designed to house them
Works by James Turrell
The most notable being
'Open Field'
Black steps lead up
to a pale blue rectangle
You are invited to climb the steps
and amazingly you
step into the blue
Thus, with every step begins
a challenge
to your sensory perception
A visit to Chichu
bears no comparison
to any other gallery

Later...
Sit on a straw mat
At a table 15 inches high
Dine on 'sashimi', raw fish
green salad
potato salad
fish curry
and shiro wine
This is Naoshima Gohan Ebisukamo
A beautiful secret hideaway in Honmura
'Oishii', delicious

No...
Naoshima won't disappoint
With its iconic, Yayoi Kusama
yellow and red pumpkins
beside the sea...

Mata ne - Naoshima

Miyajima

At first sight
as you approach
on the ferry
The Great Torii Gate
of Itsukushima Shrine
the majestic vermilion
symbol of Japanese Shinto
is awesome

Dating from the 12th century
Itsukushima means
Island of worship
From antiquity
the entire island
of Miyajima
has been considered sacred
Every rock and every tree

Sixteen metres high
the Great Torii stays in place
by its own weight
Appearing to float
in the water at high tide
An iconic image
known across the world

Rebuilt eight times
in its history
The current one
constructed in 1875
with 600-year-old
camphor trees

A Japanese Garden

City life can be overwhelming
but in today's world
where urban sprawl
makes it harder and harder
to find a place
to get away
finding a quiet spot
surrounded by nature
can be priceless…
A place of relaxation
A place to find oneself
in quiet contemplation
A place of beauty
A Japanese garden…

In Chiba City
'Mihama-en' is a lush
and beautiful
traditional Japanese garden
A breath of fresh air
An oasis
within the bustling City area

Precisely placed paths
wind through the trees
over small brooks
around a peaceful pond
The artistic landscaping
represents
mountains
rivers
seas
and forests

Glorious when the leaves
change colour in autumn
or plum blossoms are
seen in the spring
It is said
that the waterfall
symbolizes a small child
and the rolling hills
characterize life's
ups and downs…
In winter
Wrap up warm
to observe
the black and white cranes

The surrounding skyscrapers
Form a backdrop
to the peaceful walking area
A haven for photographers
Or a quiet place to sit and relax
Here is Shorai-tei
A traditional timbered teahouse
Where you can drink green tea
eat sweets and
possibly
watch a wedding party
dressed in colourful kimono
pose for professional photographers
against the lake and trees

A priceless place of relaxation
A place to find oneself
A place of quiet contemplation
A place of beauty
A Japanese garden…

Everything

Everything I write today
Is like a poem, in a way
With words that tumble from my brain
Whilst here beside you I remain

The Bear

Love is forever
A never ending rhyme
As the pages turn
In the books of time

Sunlight comes
And then it goes
even in moonlight
Everything glows

Your body shines
For me to see
A beacon of love
That entices me

The bear is coming
To taste the honey
The bear is me
I love you, you see

As

As I kiss you
The world blinks

As I hold you
Silence falls

As we walk
The world watches

And as we make love
The world stops

Know

Know that I adore you
That I believe in you
That I revel in your beauty
and your passions

You are inspiration
You create desire
In my mind
Body and soul

You are woman

Daydreaming

Daydreaming...
of you walking
into the sea
in your yellow dress
Later
we lay on the sand
As your dress
clings to your body
drying in the sun

Turquoise

Turquoise can be so appealing
Stealing eyes from where they were looking
To focus upon the vision, I am seeing

Hug

How about you?
In need of a hug or three…
How about me?
I'm pretty sure it's three…

Beauty

Words are coming
To the silent face
Passion redirected
Into ink and paper...

Beauty stands at the window
Bathed in the sunlight
Dreams lost in reality
Struggling to resurface...

Smile

Feel my arms around you
Hear my whispers shouting
Wrap yourself around me
Fill my words with silence

We cannot smile today,
for yesterday
For yesterday has gone...
Yet we can smile today,
for tomorrow...
For tomorrow is still to come...

Blue Skies

As I awake, I see blue skies
I look at my phone
It is 2 degrees
My feet are cold
I draw up my knees
Pulling my feet
Back under covers
I close my eyes
And feel your warmth

In my hotel

In my hotel
Half of my big bed
Is empty
I look for you
I reach for you
Then I remember
You aren't here

Old, very old
Heals
Always there
Putting life
into perspective
during a morning stroll
in the mist
At a lunchtime meal
Even a picnic
on Christmas day
The feeling is constant
Love and harmony

... **Avebury**

Revolution

We started a revolution, with words
We hope you listen
But if you don't
It's just our blood on the page

Shit

Shit shit shit
Shit is everywhere
Brexit wrecksit shitsit…

This government needs to sit
Upon a toilet
And shit
To ease its constipation
Which comes from the conflagration
Of a diet made rich
Off the backs of the nation…

Brexit wrecksit fixit
They need to get the fuck on with it
Before we all go down the pan
Like shit shit shit…

I was going to add to this poem
But I think it's enough already
Cos it's a piece of shit really…

Brick

I threw a brick through the window
To smash the reflection that was looking at me
I wanted to conceal my identity
From those who were searching for me

Here

I feel the real life

Is in Japan
In Manchester
In Cheltenham
In Alcester
In Swindon
In London

Here is family
And loved ones

I feel distant

'Domesticity is the death of creativity'
Josephine Lay

Death

Everything is quiet
All is still
Darkness crowds the sky
Then nothing

www.ingramcontent.com/pod-product-compliance
Lightning Source LLC
Chambersburg PA
CBHW060540080526
44586CB00012B/803